Mouth of Summer

Mouth of Summer

Poems by

Ann Iverson

Kelsay Books

Cover art: Ann Iverson
Tree, Woman, Flesh
Acrylic on paper

ISBN 13-978-1-945752-34-6

Kelsay Books
Aldrich Press
www.kelsaybooks.com

For my family

Also by Ann Iverson ~

Come Now to the Window
Definite Space
Art Lessons
Queen Freda and the Dangerous Dragon

Acknowledgments

Verse Wisconsin: "Where Does Time Go?"
"Variations on a Visual Journal" created in collaboration
    at Minnesota Center for Book Arts
Sleet Magazine: "Found Poem at Twilight"
9/11 Memorial On-line, Artist's Registry: Body of Evidence,
    Laurel Poetry Collective, and Collateral: "September 11th
    Memorial"
Sleet Magazine: "I Believe in Signs, Do You?"
Redbird Chapbooks Weekly Reads: "From a Dove"
Body of Evidence, Laurel Poetry Collective: "At the Office"
Show Me Something Beautiful: The Photography of Mike Allen
    Resnick, edited by Jenny Saplis: "Tell Me Something Beautiful"
The Orchards: "Plentitude"
Body of Evidence, Laurel Poetry Collective: "Faces in Little
    Boxes,"
Body of Evidence, Laurel Poetry Collective: "Praying Mantis"
Southwest Journal Poetry Project: "The Perfect Summer"
Red Bird Chapbooks Weekly Reads: "Mouth of Summer"

Contents

I

time scrolls through time
the zero factor becomes infinity
what begins can never end

Where Does Time Go?

Into the mouth of summer
veins of leaves
forgiveness building
a tree from rings.
What enters into time's path is eaten alive
though none will admit.
We like time since we have no choice.
Here's a heartache; here's some joy
like weeds and perfect flowers
arranged in a vase.
It's all very beautiful.
We have convinced ourselves of that.
Tell me something different and I will follow.

A Simple Dispute

But time perception
is vertiginous –
as dynamical systems of water
passing through channels
or a pendulum swinging in space:
the moment of always moving.
Then some kinds of time
afford us excess –
an overflowing residual of indeed,
certainty and certainly – as surely
as the spheres and curves
of a comet
whirling.
Once I knew a time
who every morning
left a tabula rasa
wrapped neatly in pretty paper
at the bottom of my heart.

Time Travels

And we know
which roads
it might take
on one's hand
and on one's face.
We know that time
on earth
does not have room
for everyone
so some are left behind.
What we do not know
is the road
where love will go
but spend
our whole
lives trying.

Hypothesis Truly

If reality is a mixture of dreams and rain
then the sun will climb the hill to double vision.

Perception as such is diluted
while the palpability of love

floats over the lake as a boat
in the stillness of late July.

If truth is a staircase
winding up through the sky

then a binding of book is a petal of honest
and an armful of touch

is a kiss and a coil
and the virtues of stretch belong to the heart.

Found Poem at Twilight

The moon turned the page –
we folded back the corner of the next
said *we are not ready*.
But the song was *Evenstar* –
we drove that road instead.
In our pockets we found agates.
Some we skipped across the river.
Others we kept as broken winged birds.
We flew for them
saw our hearts as aerial views
of the jungle.
At dawn, three deer passed.
One voice said
They're searching for food.
Another
I bet they're talking too.

Variations from a Visual Journal

Against the white, words are altered – anchored into space.
Winds rise up in a peach colored sky.

Angels dance in the bend of light.
Their vigor odd, antiquated.

From the mouth of music flows bird wing and orchid;
verve of song and trill are an endless orbit -
earth's gramophone unhinged.

Three sails of orange float through a red sea.
Sheets of rain brayer the sky.
A vessel's shadow drifts lone.
Water does not part
as memories board the ship two by two.

Many windows has the heart.
They remain open so birds can fly in and out.
White branches record rings of time,
measure the benediction of circumference.
Behind the gate there is a freeborn country.
Trees are groves upon groves.
Nothing is closed; even the past remains open.

Often Music Does This

In the midst of chaos
clarity's great bell chimes
the clear flight
of a single eagle soaring.

Often the heart pauses
before taking
her next step
and understands
too
that the music
has changed
but still
twirls
her sweet, soft
dress
as she dips
into tomorrow.

II

a man's mind is triadic
the content of his heart a storm

In This City

for NYC

You can fall in love
or give a homeless man
a dollar and a cigarette
or watch your shadow liquefy
amidst two looming structures
scraping sky.

You can feel the wind's reckon
from the water
dispersing answers
as words trailing down a day
that folds out to be longer than expected –
like the surprise of knowing someone so long,
but never looking in their eyes,
never seeing the goodness right in front of you.

In this city you can see what happens
on the other side of things
beyond the river, point of zero –
beyond the streets
rising and falling in its command.

You can see the blue of eyes
and enter
as if there were no other way
to come and go.
What revolves without us
forms circles on the waves
like articulate gestures,
landing perfectly like birds.

In this city, you can expand
the left, the right, the up and down.
Make portraits of the past,
pin them to a wall
these stained glass stories –
a holy path –
a common ground.

Negative Space

Study the   space around
two towers: smoke and flames
and bodies falling.   The span of bridge,
horror's face,   the blue of sky
the second plane   oh the second plane.
See the people   hanging half way out
if your trembling   eyes permit.
Their pain, their   fear; panic
takes its place –   knows exactly
where to stand.   You cannot see
the aftermath –   the air and light
around them   now that
they aren't   there.

Identity Theft

eagle lack of lore
mandate minus cause
trumpet free from Taps
man without his legs
sun starved of shine
night shorn of moon
war minus blood
human void of fear
sky drained
from two energies
of light.

September Eleventh Memorial

Of course
it must be water falling
then falling again
not just falling once
but falling twice
into gigantic footprints
where two things did not fall
but melted into themselves.
Into what deep cavern
can we make pain flow?
How deep can a name
be engraved?
How slow was the fall
when you held another's hand?
Does this water make a difference now?
Does it extinguish the burning finally?
How far away is one's real face?
How did one tree survive?
It's only been ten years.
When will we complete the world
before we destroy it?

I Believe in Signs, Do You?

If the swallowtail lands in your garden,
and not the greening down the way,
it must be a sign. Don't you think?
A message from the other world
an omen into light.
If the dying come to you
in their dreamy makeshift clothes
with a basket of goodbyes
it must be an emblem
of the world between the worlds.
Am I right?
I do not know how small the opening
between heaven and this place
or how the enormity of one
shall pass through –
I just know of these signs
and the fragrant hands
from which they flow
the gestures
how they move
what is moved and why.

A Different World

In a different world
poems fall from the sky
and anyone who has a heart
will catch one
wear it on their sleeves
so all will know
what not to say
when yours is broken.
Finally
they will know it.
In this new world
you won't have to be
a perfect vase
containing beauty only
since when your heart
is bare and grim
pretense will be a dozen roses
to fill you up again.
Irony that was once your only companion
might unfriend you for good.
Thorns carry into every world
but so does love.

After

Searching for ways to face the color
symbols to remember to forget
surrendering – easily, slowly
lifting the brush, painting the flag
walking, running: shore – road
a step behind, in-between
calling out –
preparing voice
clearing throat
raining now
storming then
melting future
melding past
tasting the slice of blue
in one left eye
missing
dreading
mixing it up
every you is you
or not
driving
not sleeping
world is moving – moving with it.

War Is in Oil

I turn the War to oil
since no else will.
Turn it to the blur that it deserves
to a time that never dries.
Turn it to oil – turn it to sand.
Twist it – turn it – again and again
make new shapes
upside down and smeared.

I melt the War to water
my breathing is the fire.
A study it becomes
a trompe l'oeil –
a mad stained stroke.

I transform the terrain –
heat
desert
blood
paint cool rivers
trees
running brooks
wild flowers.

From a Dove

Only the Wormwood Star
should carry bitterness.
Hearts were not meant
for such heavy loads.
Anger weighs
one thousand pounds
hooks itself in
anchors one down.
A feather is forgiveness
hard to catch in the wind
or hold in a hand.
It darts all about.
Chase it
through the meadow
around the sea.
It lands.
Breathe heavily,
bend low
cup it in your palm.

Section III

no such thing as true north
direction is an aimless mass

Map Quest

Drive south as far as darkness
north as far as light
en medias res
of prairie
at the wreckage site.
Drive east as far as wisdom
west as far from fear.

Meet me at doom.
Hold me at gloom
Fly me to the moon.

Bathe me in the dipper
wrap me in the sun.
kiss me in the quiet
where I no longer run.

Packing

Pack with care
the middle of the night
when bad news rest beside –
left you cold and useless.
Place it on the bottom
with your packaged lies and sins;
as awkward as they are,
their arbitrary shapes
will find their useful days.

Remember when you lost in your mind
what it was you thought you wanted?
Wrap it in newspaper
with the very moment you realized
you didn't know why or to where
you were running.
Loan it to a stranger down the road.
The times you've driven on empty –
pack those too.

Leave putdowns behind;
they'll catch up soon enough.
Label love fragile.
Rest your arm on it while you drive.
The empty container
that someone boxed God in –
leave it at the churchyard
with the lid propped open.
Pack faith. Pack trust. Pack hope.
Leave calamity behind.

Take the chair that held you
on the day you took the news;

wrap it in blankets,
the softest ones you have.
Pack up your mistakes in brown paper.
If those get broken, you'll have nothing.
The moment you found out
what it is that you can lose
should be folded with the maps:
folded – unfolded – then folded again.
Leave with your sister
the one thing that might break you.

Made in Italy

I
She thinks a trip to Italy
might heal the broken parts
with all the ruins and crumbling past
she might feel acquainted.
Though knows not one Italian phrase,
has never had a passport
but passes all the borders of her mind:
left continent, right,
present and the past.

She thinks a trip to Italy
will divide imbedded patterns
of too much travel on foot,
through the hillsides of happiness
the valleys of despair.

But she's never packed lightly,
can never decide what shoes to wear
can never be prepared for rain.

II
Only three Arches of Triumph left
and to this
remains the drizzling sky
Under umbrellas
we pile
as it pours.
In seventy-two hours
in dreams and restless sleep,
centuries of Rome
rise and fall
what seems a million times.

Though the moss growing over the rocks
and the pigeons perched on the highest column
non gliene importa.

III
All roads lead to Rome
or home,
whichever way the path
might wind.
I'll take the Trevi Fountain
over the vastness
of my land.
I'll take the Jasmine vines
all a tangle in the alley mist
and the cats
that *miao* instead of *meow*
just blocks away
from where Caesar fell.
And the tipsy, curvy stairs
of a Convent motel
a tiny temple bestowed
to our occasion.

IV
At the Basilica of Saint Peter
is where she first saw God.
Wept at the sight
of His great beam of light,
shining, blinding
through the highest
dome of atrium.
Strides took
to touch the

kingly spiral
became
restored...
renewed...
renamed ...

V
It's proven now
today-and-then-forever
that
the poppies
    &
the swallows
were hand woven
in the golden fields of Otricoli.
The rolling hills of summer too
were spun from a bolt of clover.
The clouds
in the hook and eye
of Umbria East and West
in their puffed
and willowing stance,
agree to disagree
then agree again and nod their heads
that the sky must be fringed
in the finest of soft spun silk.

VI
In Firenza
Italian women
mount their cycles
in skirts
    &

three inch stiletto heels.
Men as chiseled as the Gods
cascade the narrow streets.
Il Duomo staunch
and too gargantuan
for detainment
chuckles at wild tourists
crazy for the angle.
But nothing in all of Italy
can be managed
in a single frame.

VII
Women who like to shop
are hard core
are maniacs.
Have bought and bartered for centuries.
They disregard the ancient penis,
egg each other on.
Others worry, wonder:
Where are they?
Will they return?
Will they ever find their way?
Their backs ache.
Feet stink.
Arm pits too.
Let them loose in Florence
and damage will be done.

VIII
She longs for screen-less
open windows
fresh air,

the trill of birds in song.
Had to travel
forty eight hundred miles
to discover
what's out the window
or seventy seven hundred kilometers.
Go figure the conversion –
let the birds fly in translation.
Miles are best
in lines composed on jet lag.
They're smoother, softer
like the Umbria and Rome
in home, like
my sister singing
in the hotel shower
Arrivederci Roma.

IX
Looping circles
between
the sun and moon
we carried
our ways
homeward.
Giacamo said
we'll chase daylight
now for hours.
We did
through storms
and dreams
calm skies
rolling hills.
Through starlight
haze

the glimmer of fog.
Caught it again
across the world
between
lilac and primrose
tulip and pansy
pausing before bloom.

I Want to Live

After Lorca

I want to live among the covert lilies and pick not one
but let them own the silence of their bloom.
Want to live free of indeterminacy
and change my middle name to *summer*.
Want to dye my hair the color of unknowing
and move to a city where my maiden name is etched in gold.

I want to paint love's name a wild hue of exclamation
then feast from the dampness of desire.
Want to walk the shaded path of self
soften yesterday's edge and be a banner of forgiveness.
Want to walk in a world where silent hearts triumph
and the prize is placed gently at their feet.

Want to invent a world where the vexing, loud, and selfish
are postmarked and finally sent away.
Want a vocabulary of persuasion and a box to bury *no,*
a kite named *yes* and a sky that speaks my native tongue.
I want *maybe* in the picture always
no matter the times I change the frame.
I want it as a reference, a map, its eyes a broken compass.

IV

under shifting skies
a path of colored bricks
leads us to a childhood god
he has not changed much
but his beard is getting long

The Praying Mantis

Once I was given a Praying Mantis
ordered from an exotic bug store.
It was safely kept inside a little humid bubble bag
until gently transported to the garden of wild flowers.
I was amazed by its beauty –
how its delicate antennae rose to the heavens
frail arms frozen in the form of prayer.
It was my small object of desire for several days
but then it disappeared
by natural death or to the mouth of a dog.
But I know it prayed for us.
I know that somewhere its legs are still
in a certain, tangled intervention.

There's Always This

First Year of College

As the final bird, I stole away on winter nights
with my five inch thick Great American Literature
to the warmest room of an almost empty nest.
Between radiator and commode,
I lumbered yet un-burdened through
Eliot's, *Quartets*; Salinger's, *Love and Squalor*;
Whitman's, *Body Electric*; O'Connor's, *Rising that Must Converge*.
Dog-eared pages of favorite poems, scribbled in margins –
all examples of conflict are present:
human to human, to God, to self . . .
Tapped out meters of iambic with my thumb.
Then soft adult voices
Jack – use the biff at Mr. Donut.
She's doing homework in there.
Oh for Christ's sake. All right then.
Sometimes I muffled my tears if an ending was too sad.

What it's Like for Us

You've been gone
for nearly a quarter of a century
and it's been years
since I've spoken to you
in written form.
I talk to you in my mind.
I meet you in my dreams.
And I wonder if it isn't me
showing up in yours.

But today while driving
all I wanted to do is call –
so much has changed
so much has been revealed
we have no answers anymore
do not forget about us please.

I wanted to say to my
Blue-tooth fancy interactive
slick sync dial it up bull shit
Call mom
Call mom
Call mom.

Then Eat My Love

One night many years ago, I ran into my father at Super America. It was more like seeing a neighbor than a dad. There was an uncomfortable feeling and I wondered if he felt it too. For a moment, I wondered how it would be to kiss every time we met. Some fathers and daughters do you know. I told him about my new job and he was glad for me. Said that I deserved a break. He began to pick out the cookies and donuts he wanted at the bakery and I began my transaction at the Instant Teller. In a loud voice, so that I could hear, he joked with the attendant that his daughter didn't bring over any goodies today, so he'd have to buy something for his sweet tooth. I laughed to myself because of that tooth we share. As he left the store, he said, *See ya down the road, Baby.* And I thought of how I wanted to bake him something. Then I realized, at that very moment, that lemon bars and apple pie were the only way I knew how to say, *I love you.* So, Father, *eat my love if you must and dab up the crumbs with your moistened finger.*

Chocolates

Years ago again, my father stopped by with some chocolates from K-Mart. *A little treat for you. Got them on sale for a buck, pretty good deal, pretty good bargain.* I smiled at him for our frugal tendencies. He followed me into the kitchen and we made small talk while I heated up the coffee. He told me of his latest project of pounding out the dents in his station wagon, thought he could get the rust spots out himself and worked on the car for three hours that morning. I looked out the window and approved his work, but he insisted that I go out to the street for a real examination. I walked out to the car as he watched me from the porch, and I exaggerated my enthusiasm for the blue spots where the rust had been removed. I praised him for his work. Proud, he adjusted his belt and straightened his glasses. I poured him a cup of coffee and began eating the Chocolates. He leaned against the counter *you like those don't you?* I nodded and realized I was making him feel needed just by eating a chocolate. He glanced me over sideways from inside his glasses, probably thought that I looked too thin, too thin for his daughter to be looking anyway. He chatted on about the rust spots and I imagined him in the aisle at K-Mart, picking out the chocolates. I knew for sure then that he thought about me.

We went on making small talk and tried hard to look each other in the eyes as we spoke, but it was easier to look away. I snuck a glance at him and saw that his outline had softened – there was no hard edge just a round belly that I felt an urge to pat. Before we ever really felt comfortable, we ran out of things to say. *Well, I better be hittin' the road now – just thought I'd stop by to kill some time. Mama likes to get me out of the house, you know.* He leaned one more time with his arms against the porch. I looked at those arms. They seemed so familiar – looked so much like mine. I wondered if we had held the same things away. We had held each other away – I knew that then because his ten minutes visits caused me ten pages of words. His bringing of chocolates left me lonely. And as he drove away, I wanted to chase him down the street and call out *I love you and thank you for the chocolates.* But I was thin father, skinny of the heart. All along I held in my mouth what my diet had lacked. And for years I filled up on that empty space named fear.

Waves and Wet Kisses

I had only seen my parents kiss twice.
The first time after my father's ear surgery.
I was seven or so, don't recall the nature of the kiss
but only that his hearing was bad
from his youthful years of lifeguarding.
Or was it after he tore the cartilage around his ribs
from lifting heavy glass bottles of milk?
I don't recall.

The second time was after my mother's mastectomy.
They rolled her out of recovery.
She looked sad without her glasses –
eyes, small and watery.
He bent over and touched his lips to hers
then turned away and shook his head.

So that is it; that is all.
Two small kisses
for me to coast on like a wave.

Burning Bridges

Besides you were always leery
of what lay beyond that silvery river
though a brocade of lilacs
lined the way towards.

After it was done
you built a small boat
and learned how to swim
took long strokes
tread just inches
from the other side.
You felt no regret
in the middle of such water.

Only learned
to never put fire
to an arch of wild roses
with lip prints on it its path.
For there is was
someone walked aside a kiss.

To My Husband

Love is not a bridge on the sloping crown of water or the half-moon with apology for its lack of luster, but the ease of never crossing over that ties our lives together. I wanted to be there with the oak floors creaking and the clarity of autonomy clearly in its place. Our other halves forgiven but never forgotten. No matter what you say when I crowd you in your sleep or wake you from a dream, remember it's not all of you I want, just the face that loves me. Under the exhausted bleakness of self will, in case you ever find yourself walking there without me, remember an old song, a sad memory, my old name, and that what I choose to keep from you, must too be loved. May the years roll in and out like a piano with strong and gentle movers. Drag that song across my heart.

What Names You

After *Wheat Fields* by Jacob van Ruisdael Oil on Canvas, 1670

It was the summer that the wild lupine returned
to the far off field, unseen –
leaving no trail for you to follow.
Something left too – unnamed
while the clouds churned a fortitude of disposition.
Sometimes a child will hold your hand
as you walk away from Calamity's middle name.
The tree's tangle will spell out your thoughts
and the ripples of sea
form the shape of a heart
for rare moments,
then disperse and recollect
into something else that they can be.

Letter from My Mother

Once you've passed the gates, there are few questions to bother with. And the ones that matter, don't pertain to living. We have few memories of pain, and those we carry are of us wronging another. So, we are not as light as you think. But mostly we are permitted to store that which brings us joy. I remember the color of your eyes, not really blue, not really green.

Can I Tell You Something?

When my mother passed
she wore seven watches.
Her heart stopped beating in the night.
Her favorite color was purple –
I choose it when I can.
Tonight the pond is far from Monet's.
I spoon feed it to me and the cat.
My dad wore old socks for gloves.
I love him, now, more tenderly.
Swallows chase the sky,
open as a single kite.
Your heart might be woven
in the past forever,
but when you pull
a loose thread
it unravels.

One Ocean, One Longing, One Time

I wish we could be
something like starfish,
living without
for only so long,
growing back
what we lost
along the way.
If only one small piece
remained,
we could grow ourselves back
into whole new creatures
just living in the sea.

V

a ticket waits for everyone
the path to it
is lined with flowers

At the Office

for MA

After news of illness
in the young boy's brain
every bird finds their branch
though I see she is not able.

How quickly she darts
from a stack of papers
on her desk.
Her tiny heart is beating faster.

Her little knitted wings
barely hang around her chair,
my only sign on busy days
to know that she is there.

Tell Me Something Beautiful

for M

Say stars are flowers
flowers stars
so when darkness comes to us at day
light will line the path
as when the moon expands her beams
the sky will be a garden.
Say everything is in reverse.
Say monarchs' far off summer home
is only down the block
and the petals of a daisy
can only say he loves.
Say snow is green
grass is white
sad stories make you laugh
say tears are made from stone.
Say the fair-skinned child never burns;
harsh rays can only paint you gold.
Say everything is now rewound.
Horrid news crawls back inside
and the good
unpack their bags to stay
rather than to go away.

My Dead Friend's Umbrella

For the first time in weeks it pours;
we float and pass as passengers.
A stranger of sorts
comes to me
to ask for an umbrella.
I unlock your office
where you still linger
in the files of your tasks
the books of your instruction.

I give her your umbrella
watch it open
without you
and the young thing
protected
walks out
to brace the storm.

Thankful

For solitude and silence
the steady of hum of light
from all who walk on earth
for precarious ways of self
and the *mis* of understanding

Thankful for my shadow
for being in the shadow
the lucidity of sun
for confusion, bad poems
and silly songs.
God's grace in what we fail.

Thankful for moving beyond a pain
strength to pretend when not.
For branches exposed
their tiny capillaries
pressed as leaves in a book
against November sun.

Plentitude

Even near the very end
the frail cat of many years
came to sit with me
among the glitter of bulb and glow
tried to the very last to drink water
and love her small world
would not give up on her curious self.
And though she staggered – shriveled and weak
still she poked her nose through ribbon and wrap
and her peace and her sweetness were of such
that when I held my ear to her heart
I could hear the sea.

Ann Ivern

The Second Sunday of Advent

The moon sets her hair on fire
and coddled in hay,
warmed by cattle's breath
Baby Jesus sleeps
in some church, every church.
A friend's eyes are so sunken from sorrow
that in the pockets are stars
you can never reach
never understand.
I know there is a star
that came from Bethlehem
not sure if it is brighter
than the stars of pain we bury.
Their light creeps up
and we do everything we can
to keep from losing sight –
I know that Jesus healed the blind.
I know He breathed life into the cripples.
I know He raised himself from the dead.
I just don't know where He is sometimes
or how he grew up
or when he changed his name to Christ.

Fifth Sunday in Ordinary Time

A moon emerged and it was red.
It bled its heart on mine
and then I was not ordinary.
It cast a certain slant of light
never there before —
I reached to it to understand
then tucked away the story.
Years later,
I opened the box, unfastened the locks
to let Christ in
and God a bird
perching on a branch
became another, brighter moon
not red.

Zero Below

The full is moon
molecules fuse
to an air that isn't there.
Small droplets of the past
collide with atoms of the ever changing
against – what always changes – again.
I bake a red velvet cake that crumbles.
The oven burns off drippings of words
that should have never met air.
I put my reading glasses in the dishwasher
as if what I might see
in the New Year
could be pure and holy.
You, too, have seen unholy waters.
You, too, have given your heart ultimatums
too difficult to honor.
Our tongues pour out a liquid message;
it freezes against the pivot of land and sky.
The baton of love is passed.
What breath you have left, turns to vapor.
Ultimatums, after all, are a clutter and
melt is the only empty I can bare.

I Believe

that answers grow on trees
and as we reach
our arms extend to the highest branch.
That if you lose your mind,
you will find another
that you will like much better.
But you can never lose your heart.
It was built with four chambers for a reason.
I believe that God
is more secular than we know
sometimes a girl with yellow ribbons in her hair.
That Christ comes to us
as a small boy
in the back seat of a car waving.
I believe that sunflowers are people.
When they die,
they come back as roses.
I believe
in the first chamber it bathes and dresses
in the second it hungers
in the third it labors
in the fourth it sleeps and prays.

VI

summer swings in on ropes
grasses high, meadows deep
our shadows become grasshoppers
leaping towards us and away
when you look in the mirror
you have wings

It Led Her to Believe

She was walking through a flower-less field
when clouds leapt from the sky
and onto the path
to form themselves
into the shape of rose, red rose,
daffodil and yellow, columbine and pink,
the gold – ing gild of sunflower
who turned their heads towards her every move
because, in fact, at that moment, she was the sun.

In this very field, or meadow you may call it,
larks cloaked her in poppies and thistle,
burden and bliss, heed and abandon
under a hand stitched sky brocaded in light.

Under this home- made blue
birds sang and purple ones too
and their song was this:
She was walking through this field of clouds
when flowers leapt to the sky and the sky said
and the sky sang this song: It lead me to believe.

Dream Work

A giant monarch
lands on your cheek.
A colossal caterpillar
floats by
on a hot pink
flume-like-feather-like boat.
You write a poem
using only the letters
from a Sherwin Williams paint can.
You are an oversized
white Teddy Bear
with paws dipped in pink frosting
lumbering through a field of coconut.

Of Strangeness That Wakes

On the entrance to the mind
swings a sign *do not disturb*
though in sleep
a stranger takes it down.

Revelatory evidence
spins the blood
as the ability to recall
gathers light.

Slide to unlock the heart
so whatever
pushed you down
can leave.

Faces in Little Boxes

I
These are who we are and they change so much to the cryptic.
Change what you can, delete what you can, or try to delete what you
can't. Happiness or unhappiness is not a post. And the heart = <3
And love is greater than three. I understand that simple equation.
LOL is easy but why not COL? I'm sure you get that. I do.

II
I love the faces in these little boxes. I love longing for the real
person, when distance separates. I love that someone who I love is
Fred Flintstone. Because I love Fred Flintstone in all his clumsy ways.
And I love that someone changes their little box three times a week
and that there is an option to do so since many things cannot be
changed.

III
I am petty sometimes so sent the FB team a suggestion
to give us the option to be a girl. If I would cut my hair one inch, my
profile silhouette would look just like me: standard white woman. On
my handheld device, I am a white man for a tenth of a second until
cyberspace catches up. I am so petty. Am I not?

IV
It's been a long winter. I wonder if the birds will remember the lyrics
to their songs. I thought about posting that, but it just made me seem
too sad.

V
I posted it anyway. One response: if they make it through the storm.

Reach

Check disaster off your list
and add a sunset clause
since you might as well
have been dreaming
years before the story ends.

Stretch your arms and reach
then mount a single sky
save yourself a window seat
for every storm that might roll by.

Say you could have been a tree with hands
or a woman with silk spun leaves
or better yet a clock with legs
walking backwards into space.

Scratch squalor off your list
add a syntax of desire
then reach for the dream
that continues on
without the dreamer dreaming.

The Perfect Summer

So much sun
plows could hardly keep up
mounds lined the streets –
no room left to park.
We shoveled paths
to reach water
piles of dense, wet sun –
happiness got in the way.
Took big brooms
to roof tops –
vines of flowers snapped
from the dams:
heaps of petal and stem.
Its light leaked into our hearts
so enabling
we shut down the world
only hoped to contend
with that much balmy blue.
Alerts scrolled the screen
    . . . life is too beautiful – everything is closed . . .
We sent pics of sun mountains
taller than our cars – as high as the sky.
The day after,
we chatted at our cubicles
in swimwear.

A Perfect Melancholy

I know it doesn't make any sense
to you people who don't read poetry
who don't pick up a pen
to try and figure it out
who won't let yourselves go
into the open cave of words.
And I don't mean to judge
because I know, if I know anything,
that your burdens are always
greater or lesser than mine.
I am simply trying to point out
that, with all due respect,
I had no reason to be sad.
But the blue of the sky
and the fields of white clover
took me over
and moreover
they took me over.

Summer's Found Poem

If there is a window of happiness
jump out – language will take you over.
The distant birds will loan their wings
and teach you how to sing.
No need to burn a candle.
There's more light
than you can bear.
If something poured
its darkness into you,
go to the river
and empty it there.

To Saint Anthony

can't find them
yet know
where they were last
that beautiful bounty
of butterflies
and the keys
to their migration
a clear bell in the sky
a whistle
that calls to attention
a feeling you slipped
into an old pocket
felt its falling
remembering
exactly
where
it might land.

A Quiet Consideration on the Structure
of Countenance

found poem

If you must translate thirst to hunger
call in a fleet of dreams floating on a silver lake.
Their sails speak the language of unknown
as anything can happen on the discipline of water.

But what is aligned won't always merge with your desire
since objects in the heart are closer than they appear.
It is a fragment of your total cosmogony –
how you came to be – who you came to love.

There is a path to deliverance you know.
It could be marked with the dust from another person's body.
It might be paved with the things that you approve
and in your favor, the passerby's will nod.

Maybe it is your landscape of imagination
finally made to be with reason.
Or the tenth muse showing up at your window
with an armful of borrowed light.

Lips of Summer

Place yours
on that mouth
feel what it feels
to be the carriage
of all that burns.
Breathe in its burden.
Know the pond's tremor
as the Great Blue Heron Lands.

Autumnal

The tree lay down her derivative
in a quiet valediction
and of the water I am with envy
to have that leafy veil
wash over.
To be of such placidity
as when something of such heft
sends itself to you.
To consume that mass of rings
tangled hair of fire.

What Are You Waiting For?

After "Poem in October" by Dylan Thomas

It is your fifty fifth year towards God
and the muskrat paves its ripple of road
in a weakened sun setting forth from the pond.
The wings of Blue Heron span shadow and light
and the music of flight begins.
And the music carries the letters of your name –
and the letters carry His song.
The trees of September drink glasses of orange
as cattails of murk make plans for the day.
in tufts of feather and white.

It is your fifty fifth year towards God –
neither resolve or virtue are yours
neither grace or goodness are involuntary
but the evening lays down her dark fabric
and the bats in the sky chase matter and dart
and the moon lights the path of the night.

Towards God you have moved for fifty five years;
have found Him to be without reason and answer
have found Him to be with reason and doubt
have found Him to be with question and voice.

In thousands of mornings of rising towards God
the coyotes' high howl whoops a blur and a blight
and He finds you to be unyielding
finds you to be of consent
as the sun pours out from the eastern spout
as He moves in your fifty fifth year towards light.

The Calling

To be the sky if you were called
the river chants –
wet and white are words
reflection of the water
never mind the mirror
never mind the past intent
no one is to blame.

But if your calling is to follow light
wear a formal gown
gloves of white
pearls against your throat.

About the Author

Ann Iverson is a writer, artist and graduate of both the MALS and the MFA programs at Hamline University. Her poems have appeared in a wide variety of journals and venues including Writer's Almanac. As a visual artist, she enjoys the integrated relationship between the visual and written image. Her art work has been featured in several art exhibits as well as in a permanent installation at the University of Minnesota Amplatz Children's Hospital. She is currently working on a variety of artistic projects including a series of children's books. Her writing and art can be viewed at anniverson.weebly.com.

Made in United States
North Haven, CT
26 June 2023

38265848R00061